KEEP GOING, IT'S NOT OVER
A KNOCK DOWN IS NOT A KNOCKOUT

OVERCOMING LIFE'S ADVERSITIES

T.K.WARE with Special Guests

First Printing 2020
ISBN: 9781636255682
Insightful Creation Publication
www.insightfulcp.com

Dedication

To those who are tapped in what appears to be a hopeless situation.

To those who stand steadfast in the Lord continually.

And to The Body of Christ at large.

OTHER BOOKS

FICTION
If I Could: A Son's Plea
A Husband's Love
WEB OF ALLURE
WEB OF ALLURE: The Entrapment
Trial of INJUSTICE
ESQUIRE
The Pastor's Daughter
Ebony's Confessions
Memory Iota
THRESHOLD
Theodore ESQUIRE: The Protege
Theodore ESQUIRE: The Trial

NON FICTION
21 Day Journey of Inspiration
GOD doesn't condemn you, Neither do I
Run the Race: 50 Days of Inspiration
Utilizing Your Gifts to Advance the Kingdom
THE POWER OF BELIEF
THE POWER OF FORGIVENESS
THE POWER OF WORDS
THE POWER OF DELIVERANCE
Battling & Overcoming Self
Been there, done that
JUBILEE
The Process of Waiting
Hello Queen
Queen 2 Queen

MAN UP
Inward Search of Hope
TIME DRAWETH NIGH
Your Circumstance is Just a STANCE for His
GLORY
WHOSE REPORT WILL YOU BELIEVE?

POETRY
TRIUMPH
Soul Writings
The Writings of Epiphany
Poet Talk
Thoughts of the Forest
Our KING Lives
From ADAM to JESUS

Special Thanks

A special appreciation and gratitude goes to my Apostle S.D. James and Pastor E. L. Lindsey. These men are the catalysts of my continued growth, knowledge, wisdom, and maturity concerning the things of the Lord. I am forever grateful that God allowed me to be one of the students of their teachings.

On April 12, 2006, under the leadership and tutorage of Pastor E. L. Lindsey, the Lord anointed me as youth minister and my spiritual name was birthed. From that day to now, my heart constantly burns with compassion for the youth and for those who are trapped in the darkness of sin.

Special thanks to LaTasha Woodcock and LaDonna Marie for their words of inspiration, created in the spirit of compassion, to reach and encourage others.

KEEP GOING,
IT'S NOT OVER

A KNOCK DOWN IS NOT A KNOCKOUT

TABLE OF CONTENTS

Notable Quotes

"We must have faith in God. Faith is utilized daily without the awareness of its productivity. When we drive our vehicles, we believe without thinking about it that our vehicle will start. Even when we simply sit in a chair, we believe that it will hold us up, no matter our weight mass. Faith is exercised without even thinking about it. Faith is belief without seeing. It is trusting what you cannot see physically but that which exists spiritually."

Quote from *GOD Doesn't Condemn You, Neither Do I*

Psalms 138:7
Though I walk in the mist of trouble, thou wilt revive me.

"One thing I have learned about God in moments of trials, it creates divine opportunities for God to do His best work. His promise is when trouble comes with a heavy blow which has the ability to take over breath; it is at those lowest moments that we began to experience the 2nd wind of God. My brothers and sisters be encouraged! One of the greatest joys that comes with a knock down, is knowing that God will strengthen us to fully recover, to become more than conquerors."

Pastor Derriet J. Reed

"When you're numb from one of life's blows, look in past times and see how many times you actually rose."

Lasonia Harrison

"I'm learning that staying in the "flow of God" keeps you from getting T.K.O."

Darryl Ogletree

"We own everything. Therefore the earth is the Lord, and the fullness thereof. Now let us run the race with endurance."

Missionary Bertha Foster

A Prelude of Encouragement

You will make it! Keep saying that statement until you believe it. Jesus loves you. Stop for a moment and really let that sink in. Despite of what you may feel or what others have said about you. None of it matters. Jesus still loves you. He cares about you no matter what you are going through, never forget that God loves you dearly.

It doesn't matter what it seems like or whatever negative thoughts bombard your mind, always remember that Jesus' love for you is agape; it's unconditional. Before you were conceived in your mother's womb, you were in the mind of God and at the time of your entrance into this earth realm, God had established a divine purpose just for you.

I'd be lying if I said everything has been perfect in my life. Before the Lord came into my life, I was addicted to the club life, alcohol, violence, and the desires of my flesh. I avoided church and shunned the sound of anything closely related to God or His plan of salvation. I basically was doing my own thing, at my own pace, whenever I chose to. I didn't realize that in that state of living, my steps were leading me to a place that's reserved for those who reject Jesus and His truth.

It took a series of tragic events for the Lord to get my attention. He performed a miraculous act, took away every evil desire, and placed me on the pathway of purpose. As I grew in the Lord, there were many angelic encounters that made me realize that we serve an Almighty God. I've seen the glory of those who welcome His love, and the horror that awaits those who refuse His gospel.

As time went on, I became emerged in diverse experiences, while trying to juggle my faith and handle day-to-day activities. Poor judgement seemed to be 2nd nature. I made mistakes, but I didn't wallow in those mistakes. I went to the Lord in repentance and understand what David wrote.

Psalms 51:1-2
Have mercy upon me, O God, according to thy lovingkindness: according unto the multitude of thy tender mercies blot out my transgressions.

Wash me thoroughly from mine iniquity, and cleanse me from my sin.

Before you try to label what some people call "big sins," and "little sins," always remember that sin is sin. When you do anything, that's contrary to God's ways, it is considered sin. Having the wrong thought can equate to sin, along with other things. The bottom line is whenever I found myself in a place of remorse, I quickly repented and asked for forgiveness. And guess what?

1 John 1:9
If we confess our sins, he is faithful and just to forgive us our sins, and to cleanse us from all righteousness.

Don't count your mistakes and feel as if you're not worthy for God's love. Give it all to Jesus and allow Him to make the change in your life, to set you on the pathway of purpose. So hardship may come, people may abandon you and there may turn their back on you, trials may come in every direction, heartaches, pain, frustration, confusion, and an uproar of all of your emotions. But through it all, God's love for you remains the same. He is as close as the wind of your breath.

When we move in faith, the vibrations of our actions draw God unto us. Faith alone is not productive. The scriptures declare that faith without works is dead. (James 2;14-26) We must move beyond belief. As we operate in faith, what we are believing must be mingled with energy. There has to be a demonstration of our faith by action.

- Through faith we
  UNDERSTAND.......(Hebrews 11:3)
- By faith Abel
- **OFFERED**.......(Hebrews 11:4)
- But without faith it is impossible to please him: for he that
- **COMETH TO GOD**......(Hebrews 11:6)
- Noah being warned of God
- **MOVED**.......(Hebrews 11:7)
- By faith Abraham
- **WENT OUT**.......(Hebrews 11:8)

- Through faith Sarah
- **<u>RECEIVED</u>**…….(Hebrews 11:11)

As we move in faith, the thrust of our actions will send out vibrations that will bring what we are seeking into our reality. Once we move in our belief, faith produces the thing which we are believing for.

I remember many years ago, during my college years. I arrived at the school hoping to receive the athletic scholarship I was informed about. However, to make a long story short, the basketball coach didn't have any more scholarships available.

To compound problems, I had traveled several hundred miles believing I had a scholarship and now I have to pay tuition plus out-of-state fees, money I didn't have. I sought ways to acquire the necessary funds, but to no avail. Here I am at this college campus in a situation that seemed hopeless. I wished the coach would have told me before I left home. With nothing left to do, I had to trust God, which is what I should have done in the beginning.

The first day of school I got dressed like I was a registered student with an athletic scholarship, no special dress code. I placed notebooks, pens, and pencils into my bag, threw it across my shoulder, and left the apartment. I arrived at the school before anyone else. Once I parked my vehicle, I begin walking as if I was on my way to class. Suddenly I heard a voice call my name. It was the basketball coach. He walked up and said, "Something just happened, and I have a scholarship for you." I can only imagine what he was thinking when he saw me walking across the campus with a book bag on, going to a building that was not open.

I followed him to the office and signed the necessary scholarship papers. As soon as I left his office, my spirit rejoiced because things had worked out for my good. Sometimes we have to move as if we have that which we are believing God for. When you pray, don't send up your petitions with doubt. Faith and doubt cannot mix.

At times we wrestle with thoughts and hope to mentally come up with a solution. Some people drown themselves in work, hoping to forget about the problem they left at home. In reality, the problem never left. Even if you feel overburdened with problems, there is always a brighter day ahead. Don't allow pride to keep you from help. If you can't find someone to confide to, there is always someone who will listen and send the proper help.

When you go to the Lord, be completely honest because He knows everything. You can't hide from Him. Each day is filled with new mercy and grace. Don't allow situations to beat upon your mind. We must leave yesterday problems in yesterday, even if the residue of sorrow returns.

When we change our perception on things that concern us, everything works out for our good. Once you change your mindset, the body will follow. If you decide to trust God, don't complain when things are not going the way you thought it would go. When you trust Him, you are also trusting in His process.

INTRODUCTION

Keep Going   By: LaTasha Woodcock

In the world that we're living in today, we're all facing trials and tribulations daily. We are all in this pandemic season where we are praying, fighting, and trying to stay safe from COVID-19, effected by job loss, depression, suicidal thoughts and attempts, confusion, frustration, hopelessness, defeat, moments of discouragement and the list goes on and on. These feelings and thoughts have tried to come upon or overtake us in some kind of way. The social media, news, and everyday living may have tried to convince you to give up or to throw in the towel, but my brother and sister, now is not the time to give up.

Regardless of what you're going through or experiencing in this season, you must keep going, it's not over. We have had our mind set on certain tasks and expectations for this year of 2020, but I believe God had and has another plan for us. This season of my life has reminded me of the times when I'd make New Year Resolutions every year.

Not one time did I seek God, fast, or pray about what God was calling me to do for that year. I got so caught up into my own thoughts of what I should do. By doing this, I allowed myself to get overworked, stressed out, frustrated, and everything else. I was to a point where I wanted to give up, but I knew and believed that I had to keep going. My brother and sister, when we allow the flesh (carnal desires) to get in the way, we will allow ourselves to be placed into situations that only God can help us escape.

With everything that you may go through, keep pushing, praying, progressing, and most importantly, keep going. I know things may look a little cloudy or you may feel as though you can't see the outcome of your situation, but I promise you it's not over. God allows us to go through these trials and tribulations so that we may come out victorious, pure as gold, and birthed into our purpose. What we experience in life, those trials that we think we cannot conquer, are not for us or about us. They're tools for us to give to others who may need a helping hand to overcome their trials. One thing that I know for sure is, the seasons that I went through were not for me or about me, but to help the next person along the way.

Several years ago, what I would consider the roughest years of my life, I wanted to give up. I was faced with various obstacles such as being a single mother of three, working full time while attending college full time, spending whatever time I had with my children, sacrificing time, sleep, and energy to take care of my priorities first before dealing with anything else. I was determined to stay focused, give it my all on my job, school, family, and I was determined to not let anything, or anyone distract me.

There were nights when I was exhausted, frustrated, discouraged, and literally TIRED. I was ready to give up and throw in the towel. I knew regardless of what I was facing, I had to keep going. I had to set the standards and example for my children; I had to overcome every obstacle that crossed my path.

You may face obstacles that may cause you to feel like I did, no matter what, keep going. On the other side of the storm, the sun is shining, and God has greater plans for you. After each storm, there's always a bright and sunny day!

There's no trial, tribulation, obstacle, struggle, test or anything that's too hard for you as long as you keep God first and allow Him to lead you. When you jump over the hurdles in your life and see why God chose you to go through that season, you will feel as though you can conquer anything and keep going.

Some people ask me how do I smile after everything that I've been through the answer to that is once you realize who God is, establish a relationship with Him, put Him first at all times and trust Him with everything in you, you will then know that anything you face, can and will be conquered.

Don't allow what you see today through the natural eye to discourage you and detour you from God's promises.

Keep going, it's not over for you! Everything that we go through or have to deal with is only temporary and preparing you for the greatest season of your life.

CHAPTER ONE

Change Your Perception

The way you view yourself makes a big difference in your total wellbeing. Learn to accept every flaw as beauty. When you've come to the place of inner acceptance, the opinions of others won't sway you from achieving whatsoever you seek to accomplish.

In life, there will be some difficulties. You will experience moments of anguish where you feel as if you're pushed to the brink of your faith. Don't throw in the towel. Even if it feels as if you're about to faint, hold fast the profession of your faith and watch the salvation of the Lord. Even if you don't feel Him, He's still right there.

Everything you encounter cannot destroy you without God's approval. Before you rationalize and create a list of things that nearly took you out, take heed to the following scriptures and see the love of God. What you view as a situation that nearly took you out, in actuality, it could not take you out unless God approves. The edge of your faith is like the seed breaking through the soil.

3 John 3:2 Beloved, I wish above all things that thou mayest prosper and be in health, even as thy soul prospereth.

Psalms 34:17 The righteous cry, and the LORD heareth, and delivereth them out of all their troubles.

Proverbs 3:5-6 Trust in the LORD with all thine heart; and lean not unto thine own understanding. In all thy ways acknowledge him, and he shall direct thy paths.

He loves us that much and has a prescribed plan just for you. That alone should comfort you, knowing that God is mindful about you and has a prescribed path of expectation for you. He didn't compare you to no one else. You are unique in His eyes! The only requirement to withstand whatever life throws at you is to simply trust Him. When you're going through hard times, it can seem as if it's difficult to simply trust God.

Because the concept of "trusting" requires you to trust (have confidence) in an unseen presence to deliver you from a situation. If you haven't developed a relationship with Jesus, this task may seem impossible.

As long as you live, there will be moments that will either make you run in fear or stand in faith. It doesn't matter how many biblical scriptures you can quote or how many songs you can sing.

Psalms 34:19 Many are the afflictions of the righteous: but the LORD delivereth him out of them all.

By definition, afflictions mean something that causes pain or suffering. We all can relate, and everyone has been through the fire of affliction. I've experienced that fire and was almost consumed in my eyes, but God brought me through. I was KNOCKED DOWN, but I wasn't KNOCKED OUT. The experience added cubes to my pyramid of faith, trusting and believing that God can do it again.

It doesn't matter what it looks like, God has not forgotten about you. We are living in a time where fear is creating a blaze of hysteria. This pandemic has caused a lot of grief among family and friends. When it came nigh my dwelling, I remember being utterly shocked that the only response I could muster up was tears. I didn't understand, and I didn't want to understand. To understand why sickness or death struck that particular person would make me question why it happened in the first place. As confusion mounted, all I could do was shed tears and bask in the memories of that person. If that's wasn't enough, then I experienced a trial that pushed me to the edge of my faith.

When you've declared hope onto others, in the presence of trials, your strength can seem abased. It only seems that way, but unto every man is given a measure of faith. That portion of hope you carry is actually enough for you to make it from day-to-day. Not on your own accord, but through the strength of the Lord, and this is available to all who believe.

We are living in troublesome times and it's going to take having complete trust in the Lord to make it. This global pandemic is still present, and we must take extra precautions to remain safe at all times. Many have been affected by this pandemic, and it's only going to get worse. Businesses are closing and restrictions are placed on others. In some places, people have lost their jobs. Being without a means of survival can create a crippling mindset, especially if the person feels hopeless, in which insane violence may occur to appease the raging emotions of frustration.

For the most part, people were not prepared for the outcome of this pandemic.

When you're battling difficult situations, on top of experiencing this pandemic, it can make you want to just throw in the towel and say, "When is it going to stop?" You're at the right place for a miracle if you can believe. If you've hit rock bottom, that's not the time to throw in the towel. If you're at the bottom, according to your perception, then there's only one place to go, which is upward. God hasn't forgotten about you.

Through it all, His love remains the same because it's not based on conditions. You know how "people" are when expressing love. They only love you or appreciate you when things are beneficial for them. But if you ever change toward them, the idea of "love" will quickly shift. But Jesus is not like that. You can't alter His love. Aren't you glad? If His love was based on conditions, we would be in a world of trouble, on course to a fiery Hell. There's nothing you can physically do which will separate you from His love, He only desires for it to be replicated.

Romans 8:35-39
Who shall separate us from the love of Christ? shall tribulation, or distress, or persecution, or famine, or nakedness, or peril, or sword?

As it is written, For thy sake we are killed all the day long; we are accounted as sheep for the slaughter.

Nay, in all these things we are more than conquerors through him that loved us.

For I am persuaded, that neither death, nor life, nor angels, nor principalities, nor powers, nor things present, nor things to come,

Nor height, nor depth, nor any other creature, shall be able to separate us from the

love of God, which is in Christ Jesus our Lord.

John 14:15
If ye love me, keep my commandments.

There's an old saying that says, "Love is what it does." In other words, love is demonstrated and not defined by mere words. When you love someone or something, your actions will manifest that love openly without the compliment of words. John 3:16 days, "For God so loved the world, that he gave his only begotten Son, that whosoever believeth in him should not perish, but have everlasting life." Do you see the demonstration? The manifestation of God's love was the life of the Son. Jesus died the death of sin because of love.

When love is present, a sacrifice is offered. A sacrifice means, "an act of giving up something valued for the sake of something else regarded as more important or worthy." We all have been in love. During those moments, you did whatever was necessary to prove your love for that significant other. In the process, you sacrificed things you may have wanted, simply to place them first, as a sign of your love. Whether it's cooking for the individual, buying a gift, verbal affirmations, putting your needs aside, etc. The end result or the most desirable response is when your sacrifice is met by their sacrifice. This act of selfishness creates a bond of love that manifest without words. It transforms your lifestyle and manifest love itself in noticeable ways.

Now consider Jesus. He gave His life for you, in hope that one day you will come to the realization of His death, burial, and resurrection. In return, He desires for His love toward us to be replicated, not in equal measure, but in an acceptable manner, which will be evident to the world in word, thought, and deed.

Matthew 5:16
Let your light so shine before men, that they may see your good works, and glorify your Father which is in heaven.

CHAPTER TWO

Press Your Way

The epitome of life is the discovery and a definitive understanding of your divine purpose. Never assume you were an accident, even if the conditions of your birth were outside of the norm. God, who is the giver of life, chooses who He allows to enter the earth realm. He doesn't make mistakes. He is an intricate Master designer who views the beginning and end of each creation. Therefore, in the creative process, purpose itself was establish and attached to all of creation. Remember what he told Jeremiah the prophet?

Jeremiah 1:5
Before I formed thee in the belly I knew thee; and before thou camest forth out of the womb I sanctified thee, and I ordained thee a prophet unto the nations.

Before Jeremiah was formed, God saw his beginning and created a purpose for him to walk therein. Every intricate detail about you was fashioned by the hands of an Almighty God. He went on to say that the hairs on your head were numbered. That's compassion!

Luke 12:7
But even the very hairs of your head are all numbered. Fear not therefore: ye are of more value than many sparrows.

God is concerned and divinely aware of everything about us. So contrary to some opinions, humanity did not evolve from a cosmic explosion of particles, fusing into large quantities of matter.

Genesis 1:26
And God said, Let us make man in our image, after our likeness: and let them have dominion over the fish of the sea, and over the fowl of the air, and over the cattle, and over all the earth, and over every creeping thing that creepeth upon the earth.

We were fashioned and molded with love in the image and likeness of an Almighty God.

Being a product of His creation establishes an understanding beyond human reasoning. There is no situation that comes across your path that He is not aware of. When you feel as if "man" doesn't understand what you are going through, there is a God who fully understands. Have you ever experienced a daunting moment where all you could do was morn? In the midst of that moment, you fall into a pity party and literally beg for help.

I've come to understand that God is not moved by emotions of pity. He understands emotions but is not controlled by emotions. Crying and begging for a "situation" to pass will not make the "situation" pass any quicker. It's all about faith. You must speak the word over your "situation" and stand.

The moment you view your situation from the eyes of faith is the second the change occurs. The Holy Scriptures declare that the "trying" of your faith worketh patience. So when you encounter diverse experiences, it creates a measure of faith as you endure the circumstance. When God delivers you from a situation, it produces trust, which creates a no-so that if God did it once, surely He can do it again. He doesn't need to prove who He is, we must come up to where He is.

The Patriarch Moses went up the mountains to commune with God. Up in the mountains, the Lord revealed Himself unto Moses and brought a clear understanding. In like fashion, we must come up to where God is. It doesn't mean we must travel and find a mountain top; moreover, it means we must come out from our way of thinking and seek the Lord. If God dwelled in a house per se, the doors to the entrance would be faith. Faith creates an atmosphere, even when reality disagrees.

Remember the woman with the issue of blood? She had a certain condition in her body for twelve years. Can you imagine the depression she endured, day after day, year after year?

Have you ever been waiting for something so long and it seems to never happen? This woman was waiting for healing for twelve years. She was waiting for 4,380 days for healing to touch her body. We can only assume what the doctors of that time told her or what type of diagnosis she was prescribed with. Year after year, the hope she carried seemed to slip away. O' but when she heard that Jesus was near, something happened. Faith cometh by hearing. That's why it's critical to surround or associate yourself with those who believe.

She had heard about who Jesus was and the miracles He performed. So the scripture declares in **Matthew 9:20-22, "And, behold, a woman, which was diseased with an issue of blood twelve years, came behind him, and touched the hem of his garment: For she said within herself, If I may but touch his garment, I shall be whole. But Jesus turned him about, and when he saw her, he said, Daughter, be of good comfort; thy faith hath made thee whole. And the woman was made whole from that hour."**

This woman had reasoned within and believed that if she simply touched the hem of His garment that she would be made whole.

She acted on what she believed, despite the screaming cries of doubt. According to the law, the fact that she had an issue with excessive blood made her unclean. She lived in utter loneliness. If you touched anything she had touched, you would be considered unclean.

So for twelve years, she had to deal with all sorts of emotions and was subject to be ostracized from society. The doctors of those times couldn't diagnose a healing and ultimately left her to live a life of loneliness. She heard of people declaring the power of Christ, in the person of Jesus. All she went by was what she heard. What have you heard? Do you know that Jesus is real? If so, what are you doing to act on that belief? Push aside all the distractions and focus on Jesus. He is your deliverer!

Take a moment and consider her mindset. She had spent all her money on doctors, who probably assumed they could help her, but in actuality, only drained her of her funds. When people go to see a doctor, they're hoping that whatever is prescribed will bring forth healing and comfort. But this woman with the issue of blood, whom the Bible doesn't give a name, saw no comfort. The fact that her name isn't mentioned is quite relevant. Her condition is what defined her within society. Have you ever been through an experience and people "labeled" you by that experience because that's all they see or expect from you? This woman lived a life of abandonment by all, and yet she conditioned.

When Jesus came on the scene, He demonstrated the POWER OF GOD in diverse manifestations that the fame of His workings went before Him. It doesn't indicate where or when she heard about Jesus, but only that she had heard about the power He walked in.

Romans 10:17
So then faith cometh by hearing, and hearing by the word of God.

Jesus, who was the Word that was made flesh, stepped onto the scene as a proclamation of the majesty of the Lord. The woman with the issue of blood had nowhere else to turn. She had exhausted her funds on the doctors and was left without hope, until she HEARD about the Master. Hearing about the POWER of the Lord was enough for her to get up from the place, mentally and to seek the source of that POWER. The moment you believe, FAITH is ignited. She PRESSED her way through the crowd and reasoned within and believed that if she only touch the hem of His garment, that she would be made whole.

She didn't ask for Jesus to lay hands on her or to come to her. Her faith said, "All I need to do is to TOUCH the hem of His garment." By saying this statement, she believed that within Jesus rest not only miracles, but the essence which distributes miracles.

Despite being ridiculed by society, she knew that being labeled as unclean; she was forbidden to mingle with the public or to dare touch a priest. Her touch would make others unclean. As Jesus was going through the crowd, on route to pray for Jairus' daughter, the woman with the issue of blood, pressed in the crowd and touched Him. The moment she touched Him, Jesus asked, "Who touched me." Jesus is walking through the crowd and many people are touching Him. So when He asks that question, the disciples responded as such.

Luke 8:45
And Jesus said, Who touched me? When all denied, Peter and they that were with him said, Master, the multitude throng thee and press thee, and sayest thou, Who touched me?

Faith had touched Him, in the midst of all. Jesus knew virtue had gone out from Him.

Luke 8:46-48
And Jesus said, Somebody hath touched me: for I perceive that virtue is gone out of me.And when the woman saw that she was not hid, she came trembling, and falling down before him, she declared unto him before all the people for what cause she had touched him, and how she was healed immediately.
And he said unto her, Daughter, be of good comfort: thy faith hath made thee whole; go in peace.

As with the woman with the issue of blood, you may not be able to touch the hem of Jesus' garment, but you can touch Jesus. How? He can be touched through the gateways of prayer, praise, and worship. It doesn't matter what the situation is, nothing is too hard for God. His love for you cannot be measured. He gave His life as a ransom for many. The penalty has been paid. The veil has been ripped in twain. Because of Jesus' death, burial, and resurrection, we can now walk in the truth of the scripture in Hebrews 4:14, **"Let us therefore come boldly unto the throne of grace, that we may obtain mercy, and find grace to help in time of need."**

CHAPTER THREE

There Is Always Room For Growth

U nderstanding your strengths and weakness allows you to analyze where you can become a distributor or receiver. There is always room for improvement. Never get too proud that you shun wisdom from others. Have you ever met someone who knew everything, but in actuality, they didn't know anything? Their mind is puffed up with pride and selfishness. Always welcome the advance of knowledge, which can become wisdom for a later time.

No one said life would be easy. You will have challenging days that will push you to the brink of your faith. Don't throw in the towel, endure the moment and stand strong on the Word of God. Your strength to endure these troublesome times, which are on the horizon, rest in your ability to perceive and believe in the Word of God. It has to get beyond simply going to a church building, listening to someone sing, preach, pray, or reading scriptures out of a book. **IT MUST BECOME YOUR EXISTENCE!**

According to the scripture in **Hebrews 11:3, "Through faith we understand that the worlds were framed by the word of God, so that things which are seen were not made of things which do appear."**

So if we could talk about size, the scripture in Isaiah 66:1, "Thus saith the Lord, The heaven is my throne, and the earth is my footstool: where is the house that ye build unto me? and where is the place of my rest?"

If the earth is God's footstool, from a viewpoint of size only, stop for a moment and really consider how big God is. If the planet earth is His footstool, then how small are your problems in comparison to Him? Not that we are trying to condense God to a particular size, but If you view it from that perspective, then the hope of your petition with be asked in confidence, knowing that He is more than able. Always remember that whatever circumstance crosses your path, God is more than able to deliver you. It doesn't matter how "big" you perceive it to be. Give it to Him. Before you rationalize and attempt to number the ways that your situation is beyond redemption, consider this passage of scripture found in **Jeremiah 32:17 "Behold, I am the LORD, the God of all flesh: is there any thing too hard for me?"**

How can you say that your situation is beyond help when the LORD, Creator of everything, poses a question? We must cast all of our cares on Him and remain in a humble state. When you find yourself drifting away from His word and ordinances, quickly repent. Everything isn't everyone's business. The first person to get it right with is God. Go to Him in repentance, in the presence of error. As you develop your relationship with Him, your spirit will become more sensitive to error when it manifest in your lifestyle. Never assume that God doesn't care about you, or the situation you're in. When sin rise, quickly succumb to the truth of the Word of God.

1 John 1:9
If we confess our sins, he is faithful and just to forgive us *our* sins, and to cleanse us from all unrighteousness.

The Word of God is truth, and is the essence of our strength. The scriptures declare in **Matthew 24:35, "Heaven and earth shall pass away, but my words shall not pass away."** The power(authority) to overcome any trial rest in your ability to believe against reality when it manifests hardship. Don't allow pride to keep you in an unworthy state. His death, burial, and resurrection made you worthy! Shake off that mindset that you're not worthy. But this doesn't mean that you can live however you choose.

On the other hand, you can live however you choose, but that doesn't mean that God approves it. Your faith is more precious that any jewels. Avoid surrounding yourself with those who believe opposite of you. The more you surround yourself with negative people, eventually you will become as they are. Once you get to that place, unrighteousness simply becomes a word, and in the time of calamity, the first one you call on is

God. Some people will do everything under the sun, and at the time of trouble, they'll quickly call on God or ask for you to pray for them. Why? Because deep down inside, everyone knows there is a greater force than self. And when things seem too hard, most people believe that this greater force, which is God, can help them get out of the situation. These type pf people seek not a relationship with Him, but rather desire to only receive perks or the sap from your connection. People with this mindset have what I call, "a genie perspective."

These people with this type of mindset choose not to live for God, but only to reap the benefits. There's a misconception along the way. The idea of God and the actuality of God are two different things. He doesn't change for us, we must CONFORM to who He is.

Malachi 3:6
For I am the LORD, I change not; therefore ye sons of Jacob are not consumed.

Hebrews 13:8

Jesus Christ the same yesterday, and to day, and for ever.

As mentioned in, "WHOSE REPORT WILL YOU BELIEVE?" we must come up to where God is. In the days of old, men traveled to mountain tops to commune with God. On Mount Sinai that God gave Moses the Ten Commandments and allowed Moses to see His hinder part.

Exodus 33:17-23

And the LORD said unto Moses, I will do this thing also that thou hast spoken: for thou hast found grace in my sight, and I know thee by name.

And he said, I beseech thee, shew me thy glory.

And he said, I will make all my goodness pass before thee, and I will proclaim the name of the LORD before thee; and will be gracious to whom I will be gracious, and will shew mercy on whom I will shew mercy.

And he said, Thou canst not see my face: for there shall no man see me, and live.

And the LORD said, Behold, there is a place by me, and thou shalt stand upon a rock:

And it shall come to pass, while my glory passeth by, that I will put thee in a clift of the

rock, and will cover thee with my hand while I pass by:

And I will take away mine hand, and thou shalt see my back parts: but my face shall not be seen.

The Bible declares that the glory of God lit up Moses' countenance in such that when he returned from the mountain, the children of Israel couldn't bare it. The fact that God would allow a man to see a portion of Him, exemplifies His love and compassion for His people. Moses was God's mouthpiece. If God didn't care for His creation, then He wouldn't have raised up a man to speak on His behalf.

As mentioned in the previous chapter, unlike Moses, we don't half to travel up to a mountain top to commune with God. He can meet you at the moment of prayer, when your faith takes you beyond belief, into a moment of His divine presence. You have been given access beyond the veil. The "veil" separated us from a Holy God. Only priests were allowed beyond the veil for a particular reason, during a particular time. But Jesus' sacrifice tore the veil in twain, symbolizing the entrance to the Holies of Holies is now open unto those who will believe in the Son of God.

Hebrews 10:19-22
Having therefore, brethren, boldness to enter into the holiest by the blood of Jesus,

By a new and living way, which he hath consecrated for us, through the veil, that is to say, his flesh;

And having an high priest over the house of God; Let us draw near with a true heart in full assurance of faith, having our hearts sprinkled from an evil conscience, and our bodies washed with pure water.

All I see is love! The love of Jesus! He willingly went through the death of the cross for you! So it doesn't matter what you're going through, DON'T GIVE UP! We all have been through hard times. I've experienced devastating moments when I knew no God and after I entered covenant with Him, I still experienced difficult times. But His grace and mercy kept me! The difference was that beforehand I didn't know who Jesus was or what He has already done for those who are His people. But when I came to Jesus, He wiped away all tears and set my life on a course of purpose.

Along the way, I've had some difficult times. I've had moments when I just wanted to walk away. I've had moments when I didn't understand why certain things happened to me. I've had moments when tears flowed and all I could do was beg for that trial to pass. But through it all, I LEARNED TO TRUST JESUS! I'm reminded that, "Weeping may endure for a moment, but joy is coming in the morning." Then, in the midst of going through, I'm reminded that, "Many are the afflictions of the righteous, but the LORD delivers him out of them all." So my confidence stays in renewal, knowing that God didn't abandon me, and He won't abandon you! Lift your hands up and bring down this confidence.

Find your strength through the Word of God. You may have been knocked down, but it's not over until the Lord says so. And your name is victory, so triumph is on the horizon as long as you hold fast to the profession of your faith. Whatever you go through is for your making.

You are not alone in this battle, even if you can't physically see anyone. There is a host of angels warring and protecting those who are heirs of salvation.

We are living in a critical time that requires complete trust in Jesus, and a willingness to perform those things which are beneficial to your livelihood. If you half to stand out, be the example that others need to see. Your faith can move mountains, and doubt can create barriers of defeat.

You must believe that God is with you. For those who don't know Him in the pardon of your sins, I beseech you to RUN TO JESUS while you have time! This is not a game. Now is the acceptable time of the Lord. Don't try to figure it out. I'd be lying if I said I was perfect. I was trapped in sin, on my way to a fiery Hell, but God! When you feel as if there is no way out, God has the final word. He died so that you may live in the glory of His grace and mercy.

You have the ability to choose! So we say unto thee, "Trust in the Lord with all thine heart;

and lean not unto thine own understanding. In all thy ways acknowledge him, and he shall direct thy paths."

CHAPTER FOUR

Walking in Thankfulness

Every moment that you have above the ground is a chance to be thankful. Never take life itself for granted. Just because you opened your eyes to a sounding alarm, doesn't mean that your eyes opened according to a machine. There is only one life-giver. You may hear the alarm, but God gave you the ability to perceive the sound. When your eyelids open, make it a habit to stop and say, "Thank You, Jesus for life." Those few seconds of thankfulness can jump start your day. Ask Him to order your steps. You can set the stage for each day by invoking His divine presence.

Prayer is our covering. We are traveling down a path of uncharted territories. The dress code now encompasses masks, hand sanitizer, and occasionally wiping to protect self from outside germs. In the beginning a few people here and there had on masks because the pandemic seemly was concentrated in certain areas. Within a short span of time, it grew abroad. As if that wasn't enough, the *Black Lives Matter* movement has flooded the land as a sign of retaliation for the onslaught of hatred and bigotry toward a certain sect of people.

Innocent lives are taken and broadcast on social media for all to see, in which, deep rooted emotions are stirred up and manifest in diverse ways, according to the individual. So through it all, there has to be a way of escape beyond the bubble of this pandemic. There must be an exit into the pastures of grace and mercy.

Proverbs 18:10
The name of the LORD is a strong tower: the righteous runneth into it, and is safe.

Only through our strong tower, who is Jesus, will a way of escape be provided for those who know to call upon His name. Don't allow idle words to exit your mouth, but align your lifestyle to walk in the essence of the Holy Scriptures. Now is the time to value every day, and every opportunity to improve or establish a relationship with Jesus. When things seems chaotic, He is the only one who can bring peace to the storm. Remember when Jesus was asleep in the boat? The sea began to rage to such a force that the disciples thought they would perish. Jesus, in the bottom of the ship, resting fast asleep. When they came to Him, look at His response.

Matthew 8:23-27

And when he was entered into a ship, his disciples followed him.

And, behold, there arose a great tempest in the sea, insomuch that the ship was covered with the waves: but he was asleep.

And his disciples came to him, and awoke him, saying, Lord, save us: we perish.

And he saith unto them, Why are ye fearful, O ye of little faith? Then he arose, and rebuked the winds and the sea; and there was a great calm.

But the men marvelled, saying, What manner of man is this, that even the winds and the sea obey him!

In the midst of a storm, there is peace. We must find ourselves in that special place where we too can experience peace when things are raging all around. When the trials of life come in like a mighty rushing wind, and knock you down, don't throw in the towel.

DON'T ABANDON YOUR FAITH! KEEP GOING!

Just because a trial has come, doesn't mean you are alone. The disciples were experiencing a storm and Jesus was right there in the midst, desiring their faith to be activate; nevertheless, willing to deliver them in the face of danger. We can access Jesus in the selfsame manner. His love for us will never fail. Through the gateways of prayer, praise, and worship, His love manifest in overshadowing ways.

Always remain thankful for all things. With everything give thanks. Get into the habit of being thankful. Even when things take the wrong turn due to bad judgement, remain thankful. Jesus is still LORD and He will never leave thee nor forsake thee. Our safest place is in the arms of His care. The more you learn of Him, the more you'll understand His nature and your spirit will become more sensitive in the presence of unrighteousness. I've heard someone mention that the year 2020 should have really thought people how to pray. I agree. Sadly, everyone is not going to seek a relationship with Him.

Some people haven't made the conscious decision to devote their lives to Him. With everything that's going on, I can't think of a substantial reason as to why people choose not to. But then I'm reminded, as in the days of Noah, people were eating and drinking. In other words, they were living a presumed life of their choosing. Not knowing that danger was on the horizon. Noah continued doing what was required of Him by the Lord and at the appointed time, his family was sealed by the Lord.

The flood came and took away a population of ridicule. Think about it. Surely those people mocked Noah for building an ark. Day after day I'm sure some people had negative things to say. But Noah persevered. He didn't allow the influence of negativity to sway his mindset from fulfilling what God had told him. Did he have any doubt? Well, the scriptures doesn't mention it. But we all have experienced moments when we lose our drive or motivation to continue along the course of life.

If you surround yourself with people who believe opposite of you, within time, you will share their disbelief and find yourself abandoning your faith. Just because a trial comes your way doesn't mean that it's sent to destroy you. Nothing can overtake you unless "you" give it authority.

The moment you stop believing that God is able, is the moment you have succumbed to the situation. I'm not saying that everything will be peaches and cream, but I am saying that everything is purposeful and rest in the palm of an Almighty God, who is Alpha and Omega, the beginning and end. So I submit to you to trust not only in the process, but to trust in the designer of all processes. We are the clay, God is the potter. Every path in life that we may take, is not outside His knowledge. When we lean to His ordering, we will find our steps govern by grace and onset to a pathway of expectation.

Your new day can begin the moment you believe. When you walk in repentance, it actually means to turn from or change your course of action. Change is a frightening word for some people because it requires an effort. When you've been doing something for so long, it can become difficult to actually change, unless you "submit" yourself to it. Change is not easy.

The process of change shouldn't be feared but rather welcomed because of the outcome. Have you ever considered that your way of doing things just isn't working? If we haven't found results in our life with the way things are going then maybe just maybe it's time for a change. Maybe it's time for us to employ a different outlook on how we handle situations physically and mentally. The moment we shift to a higher plane of consciousness, is the day of our beginning. Yes, it can happen in a moment, in a twinkling of the eye! The power of the LORD is not constricted to time. You don't half to perform certain acts to meet His approval.

Use your faith but don't stop at faith. It's not good enough to have faith or hope without **embracing change**. When these three are mingled, the end result will be profitable.

Hebrews 11:3
Through faith we understand that the worlds were framed by the word of God, so that things which are seen were not made of things which do appear

Never assume that God is unconcerned or absent. He alone is the Creator of all things, naturally and spiritually. Outside of Him is hopelessness. If you're not connected to the source of all things, the issues of life can render you helpless, void, and in a down spiral of grief.

As we go through trials and tribulations, we oftentimes forget that God is aware of everything that is going on, in the present and futuristic state, all in one moment. The way to cope with the circumstance is to trust God totally without reservation.

Some people like to bargain with God and offer their trust if He does this or that. That is the wrong way of thinking, and thoughts like that will cause you to enter into a place of grief.

Our faith must be solid in hope, and our hope must be wrapped in trust. Confidence comes out of trust. As we spend time with God, we will develop confidence, which will produce trust, and this will sky-rocket our faith.

KEEP GOING, IT'S NOT OVER! There is a blessing in the press. A blessing doesn't simply mean physical objects, but a blessing is an empowerment; it is authorization to triumph in and through circumstances, trials, tribulations, and obstacles.

Whatever it is you're trying to accomplish, never allow a minor delay to completely stop your efforts. Keep going until you reach the finish line. Then, continue going, but at a lifestyle pace. You have the ability to triumph in any situation. Don't allow mistakes to hinder your growth. Just like a kid falling down in the sand, simply dust yourself off and keep going. There is a measure of strength within you to make it! You must believe it without a shadow of doubt.

As long as you commit your ways(lifestyle) unto the Lord, and love Him truth absolute, then all things will work together for your good!

5 DAYS OF INSPIRATION

Allow the next few pages taken from one of the books in *The Mind Renewal Series*, 21 Days of Inspiration to encourage, motivate, and to uplift you for growth. The entire book can be purchased at www.insightfulcp.com

Day One: Don't Jump

Every so often you are pushed beyond your limits. Like an open wound, your faith and the ability to resist an emotional outburst bleed outward. It is during that moment when you must consider the outcome. If someone verbally attacked you or trespassed against you, should you step out of character and return the assault? Is it really worth it?

Some people deal with psychological issues without the awareness of it. They have lived in a present condition for such a while that they've actually became immune to its effect on others. I have had dealings with people who yelled everything they said to someone, in a condescending way. They had no idea their speech was perceived like that. Once they became aware, they made the necessary adjustments to avoid offending others with their dialogue. We have to always take a close observation of our actions when dealing with others. So what if someone doesn't like you? Everyone has an opinion and they may not agree with yours. Everyone is not going to like you. So, there is no need to display your frustration about someone through social media. The stronger man or woman would simply ignore all types of negativity. The Bible is our blueprint for life, and it was not created to use as a crutch to justify any ill-advised actions of retribution. Instead of jumping off the ledge of your comfort zone and acting out of character, return to your building of comfort and live on. One thing to remember is that God sees everything.

Don't compromise your standards for a moment of gratification. It's not about what someone says to you; moreover; it's your reaction to their words. The Lord did not create you to become an emotional slave to no one.

Everyone will go through trying times of discomfort. You can pray these moments away, but you can pray for strength during these assaults. Just because someone is yelling or being rude doesn't mean you must return the favor. Take the high approach and your heavenly Father will smile down upon you.

Day Two: Choose Your WORDS Carefully

I t is beneficial to ponder on the words we speak. When harsh words exit your mouth toward a loved one, family member, or friend, the wall of respect is shattered. In some cases, marriage ends in divorce, jobs are lost, fights are initiated, and friendships are destroyed.

Unlike merchandise, you cannot return those words, even with multiple apologies, which really aren't needed. You must search within and find out the reason why you harbored and allowed those words to come out. Once you acknowledge your lack of control, search thoroughly within, and then pray for deliverance. Sometimes our actions are the product of unresolved emotions toward a particular event, dating as far as our childhood or another relationship. Words are powerful and are creative. Uncontrolled emotions are like a hurricane landing in a small village.

<u>Damage and Destruction is INEVITABLE.</u>

Only in time will the city rebuild from the calamity. Many times people respond with anger when their feelings have been touched or offence has happened? Anger is a secondary emotion that's driven by another emotion. When you're faced with situations, pause and determine the seed of anger. NEVER carry anger into the next day. When faced with stressful times where anger seems to be the best solution; take a moment and seek the Lord. He will render unto a measure of peace to cope with the situation.

PRAYER FOR PEACE

Lord Jesus, I come to you now for strength. Help me overcome this situation that I'm facing. I cast all of my cares upon You and ask for Your peace to overshadow me. I bind frustration right now and loose peace. Jesus, place Your hedge around me and guard me from the fiery darts of the enemy.

Give me control over my emotions and help me to discern the moment. I thank You in advance for hearing my prayer. In the name of Jesus' I pray. Amen.

Day Three: Identity Check: Simply Let It Go

It's easier to forgive than to harbor around unrestrained emotions. Each day is filled with opportunities to forgive and to let go of ALL negative thoughts.

Everyone can remember a moment in their lives when someone broke their heart. You may remember the hurtful event, but if you find yourself pulled back into that emotional state, it's because you never left it. In the process, you rob yourself of peace and happiness.

If you're not careful, your sea of emotion may stir and crash upon another shore. Learn to forgive yourself along with others. Allow yourself a moment to experience forgiveness.

If you've forgiven someone who offended you, don't bring it back up when your emotions are charged. If those thoughts reoccur, it's because you never forgave them. Release everything to Jesus and allow Him to overshadow you with forgiveness. In order to be forgiven, you must forgive others.

Day Four: Dust Yourself off and Keep Going

Oftentimes we live in past mistakes or disappointments. We beat ourselves up for costly mistakes, due to bad judgment. Overtime, we carry the burden of those mistakes into our present, which can be harmful to our future.

Even if you duplicate the same misfortune or however you want to label it, don't wallow in it as a pig enjoying mud. Get up from that place and only carry only the wisdom of the experience, if there be any.

Remember that every day is an opportunity to embrace the newness of life. A mistake is an indication that you're human, and prone to mistakes. So don't beat yourself up.

Learn from your mistakes and continue to live.

Day Five: Overcoming the Opinion of Others

Everyone has an opinion of some sort. When you yield to someone's opinion, you actually give them a type of subliminal power over you. They have the ability to string your emotions along because of their approval or disapproval. God's opinion is the only one that should matter, but that is not always the case. Many people are influenced by peers, in one way or another.

What if someone told you that you'll never amount to anything? Depending on your relationship to the individual, those words can become a dagger to your potential. Like a tape recorder, the gloom of those words will replay in your mind and slip into your reality. The same can be said about positive words. God never intended for us to be controlled by another person's feelings. Instead, we should focus on what God has already declared through His word. When you give into the thoughts of other people, it can affect your self-esteem. Poor self-esteem can lead to erratic behavior problems.

To simply put it, self-esteem is how you view yourself. When your opinion of yourself enters a downward slope, it shifts into poor self-esteem, which can lead into diverse forms of depressions and mental angst. When an individual steps onto that particular downward slope, the cruel words of another can become a violent push into an abysmal reality.

One of my favorite scriptures is found in the book of Jeremiah. Even though I've used this scripture before, it applies more so with this particular day. God specifically addresses how He feels concerning us. This scripture alone is a boost for anyone facing a difficult time of self-evaluation.

Jeremiah 29:11
For I know the thoughts that I think toward you, saith the Lord, thoughts of peace, and not of evil, to give you an expected end.

About the Author

T.K. Ware's style of writing brings a fresh perspective of faith-based books, in which he calls Suspense with Soul. His inspired writings weave together reality with the supernatural, in hope to plant a seed of the gospel. Often known for his memorable fictional characters and series, including Charles "ESQUIRE" Everson, The Pastor's Daughter, Ebony's Confessions, If I Could: A Son's Plea, and the Up Close & Personal Series. Outside of fictional writing, he employs inspiration and motivation through his devotionals.

In the words of Barry Irwin Brothpy, "Ware demonstrated that he is amongst the new generation of prophetic writers that will use the muses of writing to exhilarate others. With such a calling, Ware also possesses a humility best depicted in his own words of why he writes. Ware's words echo the callings of this new generation of underground writers: regardless of prestige or payoff, God is raising up prophetic writers to share the Gospel message through poetry and fiction.

TK Ware is an inspirational author, poet, and motivational speaker. His work has reached coast to coast, inspiring all who reads the inspired writings. He is the author of over twelve books, in which several have adorned the bestselling list. When he's not inspiring others with his books, you can find him in various social media outlets, planting seeds of hope and pulling others from the darkness of doubt. Being a man of inspiration, cultivated by faith, accolades and prestigious awards play secondary to his purpose in writing, which is to please God.

You can learn more at www.insightfulcp.com

www.ingramcontent.com/pod-product-compliance
Lightning Source LLC
Chambersburg PA
CBHW051045030426
42339CB00006B/201